ADVENTURES IN CAMPING

...whatever could have

gone wrong...

Rebecca S. Carlisle

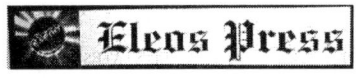

Eleos Press

Rogersville, Al

First Printing: Adventures in Camping

Dedication

You hold a special place in our hearts.
You brought joy, love and a
Strong faith in God into our lives
The bond of love, family and friendship
Remains until we meet again

Chad Rexrode
1971 – 2017

Richard Carlisle
1941 – 2018

Preface

I have had the privilege of knowing Rebecca S. "Becky" Carlisle for many years. We met at a session of Christian Writers' Boot Camp, led by writers Denise George and Carolyn Tomlin. I, along with many of the others in attendance, was fascinated by Becky's amazing story of having donated a kidney to a complete stranger (*Sharing Lives: A Tale of Two Kidneys*).

Since that time, I have worked with Becky to produce several more of her books. I appreciate her asking me to publish this manuscript.

Becky asked me to include one of my personal camping stories. So, for what it's worth, here it is:

> In the late 1970s, I purchased a canvas Coleman tent (if you have ever slept in one, you know how wonderfully they smell).
>
> After getting off work on a Friday afternoon, my wife and I packed our belongings and headed to the north Georgia mountains.
>
> We had just reached the outskirts of our planned destination when night began to fall. We pulled off at a state rest area to grill some hamburgers. After finishing our meal, we noticed a thicket behind the clearing. Shrugging my shoulders, I pointed and suggested, "Why don't we just set up camp back there?" Exhausted, Diane agreed.

I unloaded the brand new tent from its box and spread the contents out on the ground. Flashlight in hand, I reached for my hammer and began to pound one of the stakes into the corners of the tent.

Glancing back at the instructions and reaching for another stake, something on the instruction page caught the corner of my eye. Something small, shiny, and black—and moving!

Turning my full attention to the distraction, I saw that this interruption had a curved tail with a stinger at the end. I had been raised in the city, but I immediately recognized what I was dealing with—a scorpion! My hand was within inches of what I thought might have been a deadly stinger. I quickly withdrew my hand and moved into action. Fortunately for me, my hammer had a distinct advantage over my tiny adversary. Overkill was the rule of the day. I obliterated the poor creature. The last thing to stop moving was that horrible appendage.

Our camping adventure was over—or so we thought. We moved our sleeping bags and extra clothes into the tent. As soon as we were settled, we heard the sound of many loud engines coming down the highway and stopping at our campground. I opened the tent flap to discover a group of around eight motorcyclists. These were not the friendly "weekend warrior" types. Their leather jackets were clearly emblazoned with Hell's Angels insignia. Subconsciously, I reached for the only weapon I had—a barbecue fork I brought for cooking hot dogs.

Diane and I sat silently in our canvas prison for what seemed like an hour. We prayed! Finally, without ever having glanced our way, the burly entourage mounted their metallic beasts and headed back down the highway. Crisis averted.

We went to sleep, knowing that our camping adventure had now come to a close. Nothing else could possibly go wrong. Or so we thought...

Early the next morning, we had another uninvited "guest." We heard a loud snorting sound and, thanks to the rising sun and the much-too-thin fabric of our tent, we saw a large shadow circling around our extremely flimsy shelter. Our imaginations were running wild. We agreed, "It must be a bear!"

Seizing my trusty weapon (the barbecue fork), I considered stabbing the "bear" through the tent wall. Then I thought, "That will probably just make him angry." And, honestly, I have always been cheap; I didn't want to ruin my new tent.

We waited breathlessly for several minutes as the "bear" moved closer to the open tent flap. Finally, he shoved his snout into the tent. Our "bear" was actually a dog. A German Shepherd mix. He was quite friendly. He was also very hungry. We shared some of our breakfast food with him. Satisfied, he left our company in search of other campers who would take care of his next meal.

We packed everything and drove to the campsite I had circled on our map—our final destination. Thankfully, the rest of our trip was quite uneventful. But our experience would become one that we would never forget...

- Pastor and Author, W. Scott Moore
  BBA, MDiv, DMin

INTRODUCTION

For thirty years my husband, Richard and our two daughters, Sam and Shea, along with four other families made indelible camping memories never to be forgotten. Families united over the love of camping and become part of my family. *Adventures in Camping: Whatever could have gone wrong*, tells a story of friendship at its best.

We become an extended family—always there for each other. In the group are experienced campers willing to help the first time campers. At times we rely on our instincts knowing first-hand because this is what happens to us. Together we made a life time of memories and miracles. *Adventures in Camping: Whatever could have gone wrong* shares the adventures experienced by members of our camping group.

Left to right: Mike and Ginger Turner; Dan and Nancy McMichael; Ray and Gail Sheppard; Becky and Richard Carlisle; and Susan and Cecil Hadaway.

The friends who introduced us to the joys and, sometimes, the frustrations of camping:
- Mike and Ginger and their three children; Patti, Amy and Michael.
- Dan and Nancy with their two children; Leslie and Chris.
- Cecil and Susan with their daughters; Lydia, Tara and Felicia.
- Ray and Gail with their children; Seth and Leigh

Table of Contents

Chapter One

Driving to Carrollton, Georgia, today I pass a truck towing a camper and immediately a flood of memories returns to the time spent camping with a special group of people better known to our family and friends as the "Camping Families." It doesn't stop me from wanting to text everyone and plan another trip. Camping was the highlight of our vacations. For us, camping is a time to get away from the day to day routine providing a change of scenery and a way to energize and relax.   Whether it is camping in the North Georgia Mountains in the fall or heading to the Florida beaches in the summer it was always an adventure.

Our children are older with families of their own and sadly some members of our group are no longer with us. I long to recapture each memory and, since rolling back time is not an option, these memories grow sweeter each passing season. Times spent camping remains a vital part of wonderful times and memories to last a lifetime. If you enjoy camping you have discovered one of many joys which comes from spending night under the stars next to a campfire or out on the beach watching the sun go down.

Almost everyone in our group would agree some trips are adventures from hell. It is during these times we find God is there to save us and we experience His miracles changing our lives forever. Our first camping trip almost becomes our first and last.

Mike and Ginger invite us to go on a camping trip for the weekend. We leave after work on a Friday afternoon heading to the mountains of North Georgia four hours away. Mike and Ginger have a tent large enough for their family of five. They pack their supplies and tent in the jonboat on a trailer towed behind their car. We lead the way in a Scotty Camper we borrow from my parents. Everything is going well as we enter Atlanta, Georgia's city limits.

A Friday afternoon is not an ideal time to travel through Atlanta towing a camper or a boat. With traffic so congested in all four lanes and cars traveling at the maximum speed limit we are not accustomed to towing a camper Richard accidently gets on an exit ramp heading to Chattanooga, Tennessee. With all the busy traffic we are unaware Mike and Ginger are no longer behind us. So I did what anyone would do, I quickly stick my head and half of my body out the truck window in an attempt to communicate with Mike and Ginger whom I think is right behind us. With my hands and arms I began motioning and screaming at the top up my lungs,

"Go on ahead and we will see you at the campground as soon as we get turned around," I just know Ginger can hear and understand my screaming and my hand motions. The only person who could make out what I was saying is Richard and he just shakes his head and smiles without saying a word. I am still reasoning Mike and Ginger obviously see us exit on the wrong ramp. I assume they will continue on their way to the campground two hours away. A time before cell phones and we have no way to contact them. Richard knew something wasn't right, but I convince him Mike and Ginger saw us exit and they will continue on to the campsite.

Richard merges back on the highway at the next exit and continues driving to the campground. Again I believe we will pull into the campground to see Mike, Ginger and the kids setting up camp. We arrive two hours later and I go in to register. The camp manager tells me he received a call from Ginger telling him they have to cancel their reservation and head back home. Ginger explains what happened and asked them to let us know when we arrive. .It seems a few miles back Mike was traveling in the inside middle lane when a tire on the jonboat trailer blows. The jonboat remains on the trailer with the ties holding it in place. Their car shakes from the weight of the jonboat and the trailer with a flat tire. Mike manages to maintain control of the car while traveling at a fast speed. His concern is with his family in the car and their safety. Other people in the cars on the interstate see what is happening and slow down to clear a path for Mike to cross two lanes of traffic to get to the shoulder of the road. A serious car accident is avoided and it is a miracle no one is hurt. We give thanks to God knowing He was watching over us. A miracle the boat did not turn completely over or leave the trailer and hit another car. The jonboat survives with no damage and will go on many trips over the next thirty years. Ginger and the children sit on the shoulder of a busy interstate two hours from home. Mike walks to the nearest exit and calls Bud, his brother, to come and get them. They put the jonboat and supplies on the back of Bud's truck and head home tired and unharmed. It is late when they get back home. They did not know where we were or what had happened to us.

When Richard finds out what happened we immediately head back and five hours later we arrive back home around 1:00 AM in the early morning. When the sun comes up I call

Ginger to let her know we are back and how badly we feel leaving them on the side of the road. Mike and Richard vow never to travel without some form of communications device. They use a "walkie-talkie" (a portable two way radio) until the cell phone comes along.

It is Saturday and since we all already packed we decide to go camping somewhere close to home. We head to Burnt Village Campground in Lanett, Alabama a nice place to camp. There it is a compact camper for sale. Mike and Ginger check it out and decide it would be just what they need, with no wasted space and seemingly enough room to sleep a family of five and even sleep six when Mike's mother goes with them. It was bigger on the inside than it appeared on the outside. Other campers would see them coming out of this little camper and would ask if they could take a peek inside not believing that it could sleep six people. Mike had a unique way of parking this camper. He would disconnect the camper from the car, pick up the front hitch and move it by hand wherever it needed to go. Mike would yell,

"Okay, kids, stand on the back bumper."

Patti, Amy, Michael and Sam and anyone present, including me, would jump on the back bumper to weigh it down so he could turn and position the camper into place.

Ginger and Richard supervise the parking space to make sure it is parked in the camping site.

Later Mike and Ginger purchase a much bigger camper which was roomier and would accommodate a growing family and later all the grandchildren. The special little camper gave us some great memories. We only camped one time at Burnt Village campground, but it will remain as the campground where Mike and Ginger found the little camper on a Saturday morning in Lanett, Alabama.

The love for camping is now in my blood as the weekend ends and we head back home. I can't wait to go again.

The jonboat belongs to Mike and Ginger begins as a carrier for the tent and camping supplies. Thorough the years the jonboat plays an important role in God's plan to protect us from serious car accidents and times in the Gulf of Mexico when the jonboat provided and stayed upright for members of our group from drowning. Today the jonboat is retired to Mike and Ginger's pond and now rides the grandkids around the lake while they fish and play. Many would consider the jonboat just a small fishing boat, but God showed us it could withstand storms with high winds in the deep waters of the Gulf of Mexico. The jonboat becomes a testament to what God can do.

Chapter Two

North Georgia Mountains are beautiful especially in the fall. The cool nights and warm days are perfect camping weather where each town comes alive with tourists descending from all over to observe nature's colorful trees on display. The towns plan fall festivals, hayrides, haunted forests and craft shows for tourist and locals to celebrate the fall season.

There are Fruit Stands on the side of the road selling home grown apples, boiled or roasted peanuts, and sorghum syrup simmering in big kettles. The aroma and sweet fragrance of the syrup cooking makes your mouth water. I ask if I can purchase a piece of sorghum cane and they give it to me. I want to taste it because I grew up chewing on sugar cane. Sorghum looks like sugar cane, but there is a difference in the taste and not as sweet to me as sugar cane. Richard purchases two jars of sorghum syrup, one for himself and one for Mike. The owners of the stand dip out the syrup shimmering in the kettles over a fire. The syrup is poured into a warm mason jar. Richard and Mike have a plan to talk Ginger into making her famous biscuits to eat with the sorghum syrup. Richard just thinks the syrup tastes better drizzled over Ginger's warm buttered biscuits. We also buy a bushel of apples that grow so well in the area although I know they are the same apples you buy back home in the grocery store. You can feel fall in the air which is a perfect time to build a camp fire, roast marshmallows and hotdogs. After the sun goes down we remain outside sitting around the camp fire telling stories relaxing and enjoying the night.

On this trip we decide to take the kids to a Haunted Forest. Shea is five years old and wants to go with Sam, her sister, and the other kids. They have a horse drawn wagon which carries us to the top of the hill and drops us off to walk back down with spooks, ghost and goblins ready to jump out and scare us.

Shea did not like scary things, but she is brave until time to walk down the hill. She decides she is not going to walk down because it looks too scary. Not wanting to spend the night at the top I tell her it is okay and I will carry her. I find out she cannot hold on to me because she has to use her hands to cover her eyes. I pick her up and down the hill we go. The spooks think it is funny and they go easy on me trying not to scare Shea. We make it down and to this day every time I see or hear about a haunted forest I think of the night I was carrying Shea.

Cecil recalls:

> *Susan and I, along with our three daughters, Lydia, Tara and Felicia bring Christmas lights to hang from the trees. The lights set the mood and give off a twinkling of light reminding us of colorful lightening bugs. The lights give a glow, just enough light to see where you are going. It creates an ambience in the night sky. Everyone has Christmas lights and I discover a second use for those Christmas lights. The lights become special camping lights to be used to light the camp sites and pathways for everyone. The lights are a hit with everyone.*

Chapter Three

Richard, Sam, Shea and I go to Vogel State Park, in Blairsville, Georgia with our camping families for a long weekend. We tour the area during the day and on Saturday night we walk to the pavilion to listen to a Blue grass music band performing at the Park. The campground has a rope hanging over a tree limb at the edge of a fifteen foot cliff overlooking a small creek. Some of our adventurous kids swing over the creek and easily return back to the ledge without dropping into the shallow cold water. Richard watches Amy, as she easily swings out on the rope and gracefully swings back. He just knew he could do it with ease; after all he was the oldest of five brothers. Growing up Richard and Harry, one of his brothers, would swing from trees and drop into the river water close to his home. He is determined to do it again. He takes the rope and off he swings across the narrow creek, but on his return his big toe makes it back to the edge but his body didn't quite make it all the way. As he dangles with one toe on the ledge I can see the look of desperation on his face. Ginger and I are watching and hear Richard say as he swings close to us.

"Help ...GRAB ME!"

Ginger and I look at each other and Ginger said,

"I can't get wet cause I only brought one bra and if it gets wet I am in trouble."

I get tickled and when I realize Richard isn't kidding and it is too late to catch him. With each swing he gets further away from the ledge. Finally Richard finishes swinging and is holding onto a rope in the middle with the creek down below. There's only one thing left to do and that is to drop and fall in the water. Without saying a word Richard lets go of the rope and into the cold water he falls. We know the fall didn't hurt him and now everyone watching is laughing hysterically. Richard calmly picks himself up and walks down stream to our camper. I go check on him and even though at first he didn't see the humor in the situation. All he would say is,

"Amy made it look so easy."

This weekend he discovers wet blue jeans do not dry if all you have is a campfire to dry them. He stands close to the fire to get warm in an attempt to dry the only pair of jeans he brought. He wears them two more days and on the last day they are almost dry. From that day forward he makes sure to bring an extra pair of jeans just in case and Ginger decided to make sure she bought an extra bra just in case.

Chapter Four

Setting up the campers takes Richard, Mike, Dan, Cecil, and Ray chipping in to make sure everyone's camper or tent is set up. On this trip they assist Ray, who was driving a motorhome, discover the tank which holds the toilet water is open. The men tease Ray about letting his kids use the toilet as they travel down the road. Teasing Ray about what the cars behind must have thought when they saw something coming out from underneath the RV towards their car. Wondering and then realizing what it was. "Oh, no!" Not sure this happened but over the years it is told as the truth and the story grew even bigger each time the men tell it.

The men always bring firewood from home to build a campfire. The last thing Richard would do as we leave is to throw firewood in the bed of the truck. At sunset we pull up chairs or sit on a log by the campfire. We bring out the marshmallows and eat "tube steaks", Mike's name for hotdogs. He would tell his kids they are having tube steaks for dinner. They would get excited thinking they are having steak only to discover it really was hot dogs.

Once I was eating a hot dog and baked beans on a paper plate in a paper plate plastic holder. The lighting is poor from the campfire and afterwards I went inside the camper to clean up and I discover the inside of my paper plate is gone. I had eaten the inside of my paper plate. The bad thing is it tasted pretty delicious and I couldn't tell the difference... It tasted just like a roasted hot dog, paper plate and all.

Susan recalls:

We have an extension on the back of our motorhome which was a perfect size to fit a full-size gas grill. Cecil thought it would be a great idea to carry our full size grill. When we got to the campsite the men can't believe Cecil brought his patio size grill camping. They had brought the small portable grills to cook on. The other men tease Cecil and thought it was hilarious, but Cecil didn't say anything and he took the ribbing from the others. The teasing really didn't bother Cecil as he fired up the grill. He finishes grilling and we finish eating before the others campers were through grilling. Afterwards Mike asks Cecil,

"I hate to ask you this, especially after all of the teasing I gave you, but could I use your grill?"

Before the trip was over, all the camping families ended up using our grill. Cecil certainly didn't mind letting everyone grill it cooks faster and was a huge success. You learn that all the camping families will share with you too. If someone forgets something there is always someone who has what you need.

Chapter Five

Cecil recalls,

Excitement is in the air. It's our first camping outing with a borrowed pop-up camper. Susan, our daughters and I are loaded and headed out excitedly to join the other camping families at Port St. Joe. Somewhere along the way I realize the pop-up camper isn't traveling as smoothly as it should be. I stop to check it out and everything seems fine so we continue on to the campground. Still the uncomfortable vibration continues and I stop a couple more times. Finally I realize several tire lugs are missing from the tires. One tire is rolling with only one lug just an accident waiting to happen. To make matters worse it is on a Sunday afternoon in a rural peanut farming area with few places to stop and get help.

Along came a generous farmer who gave me a lug to stabilize the tire until we can get to the auto parts store. We purchase enough lugs to stabilize all of the tires and get to our destination safely. By the time we set up camp that afternoon and visit with everyone we are more than ready to call it a night. Our good friends have other plans for us.

Since this is our first trip camping it only makes sense to be sure the first night would one we wouldn't forget.

All the men in the group wait until Susan, daughters and I go to bed and fall asleep. They throw food scraps under our camper. The nocturnal animals (skunks and raccoons) in the campground enjoy a banquet under our pop-up! They are having a party and keep us up all night. Our first night would be a night we would remember.

Campgrounds lend themselves to be a great safe place to ride a bike. Children will ride a bike in a campground all day long. Leslie and Chris, Dan and Nancy's children, along with Leigh and Seth, Gail and Ray's children, Sam and Shea, Richard and Becky's children, and Patti, Amy and Michael, Mike and Ginger's children, along with my children, Lydia, Tara and Felicia enjoy riding their bikes through the campground until night fall. They kids fall asleep at night as soon as their heads hit the pillow.

Chapter Six

Ginger recalls:

Not long after, Mike and I purchase a much bigger camper and we head to the beach with Dan, Nancy, and Richard and Becky. It is always comforting to travel together just in case someone has trouble and needs help. On this trip Dan has truck problems and stops about a mile behind us. While Mike and Richard go back to help Dan, Becky and I decide to let the awning out on our new camper. We set up chairs and relax while we wait on the men to fix Dan's problem. We are on the main road right in front of someone's house. The owner comes out and asked if we needed anything and we say, "No thanks." We didn't realize he probably is asking. "What are you doing setting up camp in my front yard!"

We are a little naïve and did not realize we are intruding on his territory. The man is nice to us after he realizes we are harmless.

It is at that moment, as Becky and I and the kids are relaxing in our lawn chairs with the camper awning out and enjoying a cold drink in this man's front yard, I hear Mike yelling a mile away,

"What are y'all doing? We are ready to pull out. Get the awning in and get ready to go. We are heading your way."

It is at that moment I realize I didn't know how to put the awning back in correctly. Oops! Needless to say Mike is not a happy camper. Mike comes on down and puts the awning in and we are on our way to the campground.

Later we laugh and wonder what the family must have thought about us setting up camp in their front yard. We always meet the nicest people when we go camping.

Chapter Seven

Camping at Port Saint Joseph State Park near Cape San Blas, Florida would become our favorite place to camp. Our first time at Port St. Joe we borrowed my parents Scotty camper and it did not have an air conditioner. Richard had a small AC window unit that fit in the back window, but he waits to put it in the window after we stopped. He did not want it falling out of the window as we traveled. . As we pull into the campground we find Mike and Ginger's tent and Dan and Nancy's tent. We locate Cecil and Susan's and Ray and Gail's camp sites close by. We were close together and the camp sites have all the conveniences of home, almost, with restrooms and washrooms located close by. They brought big fans to cool off and keep insects away. Everyone helps us park the camper and get set up. As soon as Richard puts the AC unit in the window and turned on the AC, all the kids came running to the small Scotty camper. It made me feel special even though I really knew they were there enjoying the air conditioner. It was well into the nineties, hot and sunny. The breeze made it perfect beach weather.

On our first night Amy sleeps in the camper on the top bunk with Sam. During the night Amy gets sick. Richard and I are on the bottom bunk directly under the top bunk. Amy gets down during the early morning hours without waking us and went back to her campsite. Amy told her mom and dad she got sick and she thinks she may have thrown up in the camper. Mike gets up and comes over to our camper to see if we need him to help clean up. Mike knocks on our door several times to wake us up, Mike said,

"Richard, wake up Amy is sick. Do you need me to help clean up?

"Just a second Mike and I will open the door." said Richard.

I wake and try to figure out how Mike knows Amy is sick, I still think Amy is still in our camper. Richard gets up to let Mike in and that's when he makes the discovery. His shoes are on the floor beside the bunk and as he slips them on and realizes what is in his shoes. He knew it could happen to anyone and he thought it was hilarious. Richard would try to get back by teasing Amy every chance he got but somehow Amy always got the best of anything he tried to do. She enjoyed scaring Richard by swimming under water and grabbing his ankle without him knowing she was anywhere around. Richard would scream and run through the water. We laughed every time. It was just funny, even after the hundredth time to see Richard getting scared by Amy. Amy moved like a cat, very quiet.

Chapter Eight

Dan recalls:

When Nancy and I started camping our children were young. Leslie our daughter was about seven and Chris was a toddler. At the time Chris was the youngest and not big enough to ride a bike. He would ride his tricycle. Chris tried to keep up with the big kids on their bikes and he couldn't go fast enough. We all felt badly for Chris, but he grew and the next year when we went to the beach he rode his bike. Years later Leslie and Chris are all grown up and married with families of their own I am standing looking outside the camper door and there goes my grandson, Caleb, Leslie and Clif's son, riding his tricycle and it brought back memories of Chris at that age.

We continue to go to our usual camp site in Port St. Joe, Florida. Leslie and her husband, Clif enjoy camping and go with Nancy and me. Leslie and Clif have four children. Sammy, our youngest granddaughter is almost fifteen months old and her first time at the beach. It is a treat watching her and seeing everything for the first time at the beach. Everything is new as she rolls around in the sand.

Nancy and I laugh as she reminds us of a sugar coated donut. She is covered in sand from the top of her head to the bottom of her feet. She didn't have a spot on her body that wasn't covered in sand including her hair. Ever since that trip she loves going camping especially to the beach. I forgot what it was like to see the beach for the first time. Watching her for the first time at the beach I remember Leslie and Chris, our children going to the beach and just the beauty of God's creations. Time goes so fast, but memories last forever.

Through camping as a family we are able to share the outdoors in a way only camping can provide. Camping takes us away from the normal routine of work and school and leaves us in a safe environment surrounded by wild life. Skunks, raccoons and deer were residents of Port St. Joe along with the snakes you can see as we walk on the beach. Rule of thumb if you leave them alone they wouldn't bother you.

On one occasion, Dan is fishing from the beach. Mike joins him and catches a fish. Not realizing Dan is close behind him. Mike throws the fish back out of the water, still hooked to the fishing line, and hits Dan in the face with a pretty big fish. It knocks Dan silly, stunning him. Mike feels awful and for those around it is hard to keep from laughing. Dan wears a fish print on the side of his face for a few days but it doesn't break the skin and he is okay. It looks like a scene from a movie. It is a good thing Dan and Mike are friends and they remain good friends to this day.

You just never know what you will find on the beach. We walk the beach looking for sea shells and sand dollars. I have collected some beautiful conch shells and sand dollars in the bay to add to my collection. We take a big tractor tire inner tube to use as a float. The kids climb aboard and dive into the water or just float along with six to eight kids hanging on to the side talking. They would catch as many waves as possible; they can be heard laughing, echoing the sweetest sound of children laughing and enjoying themselves without a care in the world.

One day, Michael, Sam, Leslie and Chris and some other kids walked down the beach. They came running back, so excited.

"We just saw Jesus on the beach." They said.

We decided to check out their story. Sure enough high up on one of the sand dunes was a young man dressed in a long flowing white gown. He had a beard and long hair and looked like Jesus to me too. You just never know who you

see at the beach.

PICTURES

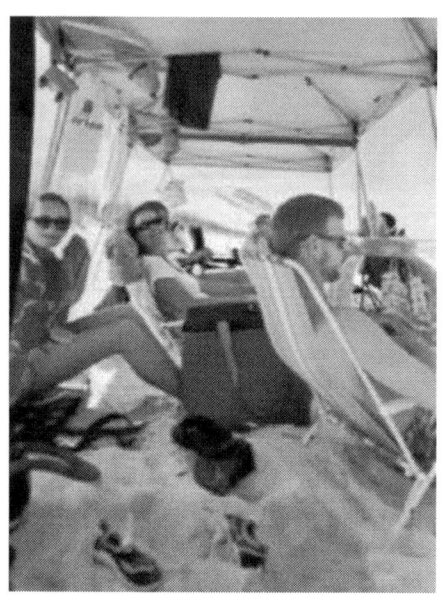

Chapter Nine

Mike recalls:

One day Lamar, my brother-in-law, Richard and I decide to go fishing using my twelve foot jonboat with a 10HP Johnson motor. We decide it is big enough to use in the bay between Cape San Blas and Port St. Joe, Florida. We fish closer to the Port St. Joe side of the bay, where the fish are biting and I try to stay out of the rocky turbulent waters in the Gulf of Mexico. We are enjoying the warm day with a breeze to keep us cool. We are catching lots of fish when we notice a storm brewing in a distance. The storm is heading our way from the ocean side of Cape San Blas. I want to head back immediately, but Richard and Lamar want to keep fishing a little longer since the storm appears way off in a distance.

By the time we realize the storm is much bigger than we originally thought, it is quickly moving right towards us. I quickly start the boat pointing it in the direction of the Cape. Now there is no way to avoid hitting the storm head on. The violent storm and the small jonboat are on the same collision path. The jonboat which seems adequate earlier now seem so small and not equipped to take on a full blown storm.

Almost immediately the storm is on top of us, engulfing the boat with high winds and rain. The waves are going over the sides of the boat. I am timing the engine speed with the waves to keep from capsizing. Trying to keep the boat upright is a struggle even with Lamar and Richard balancing their weight. Richard is in front getting soaking wet from the spray of the waves. Lamar positions himself in the middle, praying earnestly, while I am working the throttle on the engine and bailing water with a drinking cup but it is taking on water.

After what seemed like hours we make it slowly back to a cove, an area where the water is calm. The storm came fast and left just as fast. As I start the boat motor I realize the propeller is stripped on the shaft and I can only go slowly back to the dock. If the propeller had stripped when we were in the storm we would have capsized and the boat would have sunk. As we rest and catch our breath we thank God for bringing us through the storm and keeping us safe.

Chapter Ten

Mike recalls:

Port Saint Joseph State Park became the camping families' favorite place to camp in the summers. We walk around the camping area looking at the other campers and take notes on the best camping sites for us when we make reservations for the next year. As we pass the dumpsters, we notice a rug someone has thrown away. The rug has seen better days and is worn out. We laugh and can't blame someone for throwing it away. Another thing we have in common is we are scavengers and would usually take things people threw away, fix it up and use it again, but we all agree we would leave this rug alone. We even joke about someone getting the nasty rug. Everyone laughs. Even Richard. As we teased Richard about how he could use it, he said, "No way was he going to get that rug."

Everyone laughs except Becky who wants the rug. A piece of carpet to place outside her camper to keep the sand from getting inside. Becky wants a piece of carpet and here it is for free. She tries to convince Richard she could clean it up. They discuss the rug later that night. Richard tries to talk Becky out of wanting the nasty rug. Richard knew Becky was never able to pass up something free and to her she couldn't believe someone would throw away something which still had value.

Richard told me about a time before the nasty rug when Becky found a perfectly good tricycle with only two wheels at the dumpsters. Richard never found another wheel to go on the tricycle and after a year of looking went on and threw it away again. He recalled the time Becky found four old saddles someone had thrown away and he had said no way, "Becky, we do not even have a horse."

Only to discover I came along after Becky and took the saddles home and put them on wooden sawhorses for the kids to play on. That night, Richard and Becky stopped by the house and there are the saddles she saw at the dumpsters. The saddles were hours of fun for Patti, Amy, Michael, Sam and any kid that stopped by the house. This time Richard tried to talk Becky out of the nasty old rug, but he couldn't convince her.

"No. We do not want a nasty old rug."

Becky thought Richard wasn't going to let her have the rug, but early the next morning Richard went to the dumpster and got the rug and surprised her. Without saying a word he ties the nasty old rug to the tongue of the camper. Becky takes the rug home and cleans it up as best she can and uses it for several years thereafter. Everyone has a good laugh when they see it tied to the camper and we never let Richard live it down. He takes it in stride and laughs about it with us.

Chapter Eleven

Early in the day the park rangers notify us of a strong riptide (undertow) occurring off the beach at Port St. Joe. The men decide to go into the water with the children and keep them away from the riptide area. All the children are shown the area to avoid and warned of its dangers. The children are playing on the beach, a good distance away from the riptide. Some of the kids are riding the large tractor inner tube. The men are in the water, supervising and helping the kids get on the tube and watching them ride the waves back to shore.

Susan recalls:

> *I am at the campsite getting ready to head down to the beach when I hear a commotion coming from the beach. I run to the beach and when I get there everyone is out of the water. I am not sure what is happening as I look for Cecil. At first glance I do not see him. Then I see him on the beach with his head in his hands. I said, "Cecil, what happened?"*

Cecil begins to tell me that one of the children in our group floated down the beach into the riptide. Cecil said,

The child is no match for the strong undercurrent. Michael, Mike and Ginger's son, sees what is happening and realizes his friend is in danger and immediately swims to him. Michael is no match for the strong pull of the riptide and now both boys are in danger. Both boys are struggling to get out of the riptide. I get to them as fast as I can, holding them above water as the strong force of the water pulls us further out. Mike sees me struggling and yells for me to let Michael go. Michael swims to his dad as Mike swims to Michael. I see Mike get Michael allowing me a foothold to get away and make it to the beach."

I watch as Cecil regains his strength and we walk back to the campsite as he recalls the rest of the miracle.

"I am so weak after I let go of Michael. I did not know how long I could hold on to both boys. The force of the water is so strong. When I see Mike get Michael, I know he is safe. At that moment I didn't have the strength to continue, I really thought I was going to drown. As I continue to try to fight the strong current, I am losing the battle along with a very scared little boy and no way to calm him. I didn't want to give up, but I had nothing left in me to fight... Each time I went under, I did not know if I was going to come back up. My strength was gone. All of a sudden as the child goes under the water the last time,

I hear him say, "Help me, help me."

It is his voice, but his eyes are the eyes of Jesus looking straight into my eyes. It is at that moment everything changes and the force of the riptide releases its grip on us. Tired and exhausted, we walk out of the water and back on the beach. I felt the hand of Almighty God. He saved us.

*****

Prayers are said that night thanking and praising God for saving the boys and Cecil. Everyone went out the next day with a renewed sense of praise and thanksgiving for what God did. Not only did Cecil experience a miracle but so did the other members of our group. No doubt God was there and without Him this story would have ended differently. It changed the lives of all those present, including me.

Chapter Twelve

Dan recalls:

We head to Port St. Joe with Leslie, our daughter and her four children. Clif, her husband, has to work and wasn't able to come along on this trip. Thirty minutes from home the bicycle rack on the back did a nose dive and two bicycles belonging to our two oldest grandchildren are damaged. We stop at Walmart in Eufaula, Alabama to buy bicycle parts to repair the crippled bikes but the parts cost as much as a new bike. We end up buying a new bike for our grandson and using a collapsible bike we already had for our granddaughter.

We are barely back on the road again until we have a tire blow on the trailer just south of Marianna, Florida. Fortunately this happens in an area with a good road shoulder where we can pull off the road and change the tire and we are on the road again. Two hours later we pull into the Port St. Joe campground. We set up camp in a dimly lighted camp site. The next day we go into town to buy a spare tire. It is a good week at the beach, with the summer weather we have become accustomed to—hot and sandy.

The air conditioner dies in the travel trailer, but we figure out way to manually make it work. We take a different route home traveling north out of Tallahassee, Florida. A concerned driver pulls alongside our truck blowing his horn pointing to our camper.

"You have a flat tire! " He said.

Pulling over we use the spare tire we purchased, change it and we are back on our way. This is getting ridiculous and almost funny. What are the chances? We find a local tire shop that checks all our tires and he recommends we purchase all new tires. We didn't have a choice, not wanting to take a chance of having another flat tire. We spend several hours in the waiting room. Our grandchildren and daughter take the wait in stride. They view it as another adventure with their grandparents. We make it back home without any more problems. I research the tires placed on travel trailers and end up replacing the tires with only American-made tires and I never had any further trouble with tires.

Chapter Thirteen

Mike recalls:

Ginger and I are traveling behind Chad, our son-in-law and Amy, our daughter. Patti, our daughter and our grandchildren are riding with us to Port St. Joe and I notice one of Chad's tires on the camper is going flat. We are in Phenix City, Alabama and we stop to get it repaired. Ginger and I wait with the grandchildren. It didn't take long to repair the tire and we are on the road again heading to Dothan. Just south of Dothan I see a tire rolling down the highway beside Chad's camper before realizing the tire came off of their camper. The tire came to a halt in a stand of palmetto plants.

I decide to go after the tire in the palmettos. As I raise the tire up, I hear the sound of the biggest rattlesnake. Not wasting any time, I take off—jumping and running. My heart is pounding out of my chest. Ginger and the grandkids are wondering what is happening to me. I was moving like the wind. I check it out after I calmed down to discover the rattlesnake turned out to be air coming out of the tire and it sounded just like a rattlesnake. The kids got a big laugh and enjoyed knowing their granddaddy still had "it" and could move faster than lightning. Chad and I examined the problem with the tire and found the lug nuts were slowly coming off and had ruined the tire lugs on the drum.

I have always found people to stop and see what they can do to help us when we are traveling. I would like to think it is nice people who want to help. People stop to inquire, but they do not know how to help. The only solution we come up with is to let Ginger and me take Chad and Amy's children, Madeline and Andrew, Patti and her children, Katie and Ryan, on to Cape San Blas. Chad and Amy will stay with the camper and we will come back for them with one of our camper's tires and drum.

We arrive two hours at the campground after dark. Patti helps me take the tire and drum off my camper. Ginger stays with the grandchildren while Patti and I drive two hours back to get Chad and Amy. We put the tire on the camper and drive two hours back to the campground.

The next morning Chad orders a drum to fit his camper and has it shipped to the campground for the trip back home.

Becky recalls, "Other than almost being bitten by a fake rattlesnake, we enjoyed a great week of fun at the beach."

There are snakes at Port St. Joe and everyone seems to spot them from time to time. Sam, my daughter, tells me she sees them all the time.

"Sam, I have never seen a snake in the campground and you know how many times we have camped here," I said.

"Mom, look over there next to the path where you just walked and tell me what you see," said Sam.

You guessed it. There, sun bathing, is a four-foot snake. There is no telling how many snakes I have passed and just didn't see them. They blend in so well with their environment. Animals are protected in state parks and roam freely. Deer are everywhere grazing like sheep. They do not run as you pass on your bike or while driving in your car.

The boldest of the animals are the raccoons. They did not show any signs of being afraid of humans. We learn to put things under lock and key to keep raccoons from getting it. A raccoon's small paws can get into almost anything left outside. It is not unusual to wake up and find an ice chest that had been tied down with ropes empty.

Skunks are full time residents of Port St. Joe. Skunks only spray if you scare or startle them and they walk freely in the camp sites. From time to time you can smell where a skunk has sprayed an area. When they cross your path, give them the right-of-way. The sea turtles are the most exciting sea animals, and will lay their eggs on the beach at certain times of the year. The park ranchers give you a piece of red cellophane to place over your flashlights or phones so as not to disturb them if you go to the beach after dark. The park rangers place wood cages around the turtle nest so you can spot the nest. Kids are taught to respect the turtles and all other wild animals in the Park. There were many sea creatures, sand crabs and jelly fish in the water and on the beach. Dolphins and sharks can be seen off the shore. There are alligators in the bay along with sharks but I never had an encounter with one. It crossed my mind when Ginger was scalloping and something was going right before her eating and clearing the area. She doesn't see it, but she doesn't linger in the water when she realizes she feels danger lurking.

A favorite pastime is scalloping for bay scallops. During certain times the scallops float in the bay in knee-deep water. You just go out and pick them up and a boat is not needed. The rest of the year they stay out in the ocean for boats with nets to harvest them. There is an art to finding the scallops and so much fun. You must wear old shoes to protect you from stepping on a sea urchin. The local bait shops will sell you what you need and answer any questions.

As you float around, you can spot scallops sitting up in the grass and you will see blue iridescent eyes around the inside edge of the shell which looks like a Shell gas sign.

The most dangerous animals are the ones you can't see hiding in the swamp or the ones in the bay or ocean under water. We never discovered what was in the water with Ginger and me. It was enough to make us get out of the water and it made Ginger never want to scallop again. The animal that once you see it would be too late to escape its jaws.

Shape of scallop shells

Scallop resting in the grass

Chapter Fourteen

Ginger recalls:

We start our snorkeling adventures while camping at Port St. Joe State Park. I float face down just relaxing looking for a scallop in the water when I happen to float over a blowfish. It puffed its ugly little body scaring me so badly I almost drown in a foot of water. I scare Becky who is snorkeling close by. She has no idea what is happening to me and she follows my lead to run and scream. I never moved so fast screaming and dancing on water. I am teaching Becky the proper way to snorkel for scallops and she learns fast how to move if something gets after her in water. After our breathing got back to normal we calm back down and I realize I probably scared the poor blowfish to death.

Picking up my first scallop was an experience too. The scallop was sitting in the grass looking at me. I scoop it up and stand up admiring it when all of a sudden it spits water and sputters. I sling the scallop half way across the bay before I realize what I did. My first scallop is gone. The more I snorkel for scallops, the better I become at finding them in the water. We finish the afternoon with a bucket full of scallops. Picking up the scallops is the fun part.

Afterwards we return to the camp site, eat a quick lunch, grab our folding chairs and the scallops and go back to the marina to spend a few hours shucking scallops. The first time we try to open a scallop shell we couldn't get it open. Thankfully someone shows us the proper way to open a scallop using a scallop knife. You run the knife under and around the membrane. It opens and then you sling everything in the shell in a big bucket to dispose of when you finish. What remains in the shell is a beautiful white bay scallop. Scoop it out with a spoon and place it in a bowl with ice. Easy—once you know how to do it. We clean a five-gallon bucket of scallops and if we are lucky we will have a quart of scallop meat. That would be our dinner with each family preparing their scallops and gathering together to eat. We prepare dishes to go with the scallops making it worth the time and effort. Four out of five campers agree that the Port St. Joe bay scallops are the best in the world.

Later we learn the scallops are more plentiful in the bay area near town and we drive and park on the roadside and walk a mile or two into the bay with nothing but kids and scallop nets. We are enthusiastic on the walk in but, after a few hours in the hot blazing sun with nothing to drink with our nets full of heavy scallops and hungry, tired kids, we have enough. The walk back to the trucks seems to take hours walking in knee-deep water wearing old shoes. We have to wear shoes in case we step on a sea urchin. After a few years we bring our boat and canoes which makes it easier.

Scalloping can be dangerous. One trip out in the bay, Lamar, my brother-in-law, and I are snorkeling and before we realize it we drift out into very deep water. We have our tennis shoes on and are carrying heavy scallop nets on our arms and we can't touch bottom. Lamar starts struggling to stay above water. I managed to get Mike's attention and he brings the boat and saves Lamar from drowning.

Another time I am snorkeling and as I float above the knee-deep water it appears something has just been there right before me. The grass in the water limits my vision and even through the water is clear I cannot see much around the grass. It is an eerie feeling of danger. Whatever it was made me stop and quickly get out of the water. I always wonder what was there with me and I just couldn't see it but it could see me. Whatever it was cleared the area of scallops.

Chapter Fifteen

Richard and I purchase a new camper and head to Port St. Joe the very next week. We didn't read the manual; the dealer gave us a quick operational run-through since this wasn't our first camper. After all, we kind of operated from the "seat of our pants" and Richard knew how to do the necessary things we needed. We are set to pack up and go back to Port St. Joe with everyone. The salesman never said anything about the keys being different for the front and back door. We had two sets of keys. One night I picked up a set of keys and we left the other set of keys locked in the camper along with the camper manuals. When we came back, the keys wouldn't unlock either door. We didn't really want to break the doors to get inside. The first person we saw was Chad, Amy's husband. He said he would help us. He brings Andrew his son and comes to our camper. After checking the keys, Chad couldn't get into the camper either. Chad wouldn't give up and he had a solution. He went around to the emergency window and pops the window out. He then lifts Andrew up and puts him through the window.

Andrew goes and opens the door from the inside. Chad then screws the emergency window back into place. The problem was solved. Chad was always ready to jump in and do what needed to be done to help not only us but he would help anyone in need. Chad could turn problems into situations and then turn them into solutions always with a smile.

On another trip to Port St. Joe, Chad and Amy and the kids camp between us and Ginger and Mike. Chad and Mike renovated a pop-up camper and it looked like new. They brought everything except an inside lamp. We had an extra lamp and were so happy to let them use it. We always relied on Chad and Amy and it was nice to be able to do something for them.

Chad and Amy went scalloping with Richard, Shea and me one afternoon. Chad wanted Andrew to experience finding scallops and Richard wanted Shea to experience the thrill of finding scallops. It is a relaxing afternoon and I know Shea had a good time.

On the beach Chad and Amy brought the game bocce Ball. Our games usually consist of card or domino games and it was fun to play a game on the beach sand. One afternoon I played and watched Chad and Amy and the kids played bocce ball with Richard and the others.

Richard had the best time playing bocce Ball that afternoon on the beach. We had so much fun I purchased the game when I got back home only to discover it wasn't as much playing the game that I enjoyed, but whom we were playing the game on the beach with that made it so much fun.

Chapter Sixteen

Dan recalls:

Trips down to the beach are usually uneventful. On this trip our Ford Bronco is having difficulty pulling a 32ft travel trailer. We are two hours from home, right outside of Eufaula, Alabama, limping along to an Auto Zone store parking lot. We discuss with the other camper men whether to continue to the beach, return home or think of another solution. The result was a combination of the three.

We load our two teenage kids and as much camping gear into the vehicle and travel trailers of our friends to continue on to Port St. Joe. We leave our travel trailer in the parking lot to pick up when we return the next week. We limp back home—taking about three hours—since the Bronco is running on only half of the cylinders firing.

We make it back home and transfer the balance of our belongings into our van and throw in an old green Army surplus GP tent along with a couple of large white tarps. All this takes about two hours and we make a beeline to Port St. Joe taking another six hours. We arrive at camp well after dark and proceed to erect the tent in a stifling, muggy, insect-filled, no wind in sight, summer night. A six-hour trip took thirteen hours. We have reservations for a week with the days unbearable in the tent and the nights not much better. We placed an AC unit slightly off the ground with the tent draped around it. We have a fan that helps moved the air in the tent. It is beginning to be bearable, but the sand in the tent is something else and those around knew how much I detest sand. Another friend lends us a broom to help keep the sand down to a minimum.

We last five of the six nights. The cool ocean breezes, allowing us to stay in the tent at night stopped. The strong breeze cools the tent keeping the mosquitoes and no-see-ums at bay. When the breeze stops, the insects descend upon us like a horde of bloodthirsty vampires. We lasted as long as we could until 11:00 p.m., when we decided enough was enough. We break camp and are soon in air-conditioning driving north for the next six hours with very little traffic and the kids sleeping on the top of the tent and all the camping gear that we stuffed in the van.

To this day, the aroma of old green Army canvas brings back memories...

Chapter Seventeen

Mike recalls:

Summers were spent camping in Florida. This summer I took my twelve-foot jonboat with a 1-½ HP boat motor so we could fish in the bay. On a sunny hot afternoon I took Richard and Dan fishing in the bay. I had modified the carburetor on the motor and adapted the motor with a chainsaw carburetor...

We were fishing and catching fish each time we drifted over a school of fish. I would crank the engine and pull the boat on one side of the school of fish and let the wind blow over the fish. Richard and Dan were having a great time, but each time I stopped the engine I had to put the carburetor back on and hold it in place while driving the boat. As we arrived back to the dock the carburetor fell off in my hand. We came close to being stranded in the bay. Getting back without a motor would have taken us forever, but we made it back to dock without any other problems.

Richard, Dan and I looked at each other and burst out laughing. When we got back to camp, I took the boat motor off and threw the motor in the dumpster. It had been a good one over the years, but I didn't want to push it any longer. It was time to let it go.

Chapter Eighteen

As Richard's health declines, I sense this will be our last camping trip together with the camping families. Shea helps me load Richard's motorized scooter on the back of the truck. Richard wanted badly to go and to be with our camping families. He didn't feel much like going but he insisted on wanting to spend time with friends who had become family. He was walking, but tired easily. The scooter would help him get to the beach and to the other camping family's camp sites.

We got off to a late start arriving at 2:00 in the morning. Not wanting to wake anyone we parked the camper near the bath house until daylight before parking the camper in place. The first person we saw was Amy. Richard and Amy talked about all the times they had been camping and the sweet memories over the years. It had been only a few months since we lost Chad. Our hearts are breaking and we want to be there for Amy, Andrew, and Madeline. We just wanted to be with the ones we had shared so many special times camping.

Mike put the canopy tents close to the boardwalk so Richard wouldn't have to walk on the deep beach sand. This meant so much to Richard since he knew Mike liked to set up closer to the ocean. The sun is coming out and it looks like it is a beautiful day on the beach. During the days we sit together on the beach and watch the kids play. Mike and Ginger bring out the boiled peanuts enough for everyone.

The weather for the week is wetter than normal. During the night it rains so much, the water begins to cover the camper tires—only inches away from the doorway of our camper. The campers in tents pack up and leave. Amy knocks on our door to see if we are okay. All the years we camped at Port St. Joe we had never seen anything like this before. I was outside our camper when I hear the park ranger on the intercom, "Storm expected to come on shore by morning… EVACUATE!!!"

Once again, we pack quickly and leave driving most of the night arriving home early in the morning. The hurricane did make land fall and washed the park away. We never got to go back again, nor did we get to go camping with the group. Richard, on November 10th, went to the hospital for a routine checkup. During the night he passed away. I leave the hospital around 4:00 a.m. to come home. I go by and pick up our daughter, Sam. As we pull into the driveway, the camping families are lining my drive waiting on us. The closest family lives over an hour away and they must have come immediately. It was the worst day of my life. I was dreading going home to an empty house. They will never know how much it meant to see them when I arrived home. The camping families have always been there for weddings, birthdays, funerals, the good times and the bad times.

The next year I sell the camper to two families with small children. They plan to start their own family traditions. The excitement in their voices sounded familiar, and it seems like yesterday we sounded the same way. They came to pick up the camper early one Sunday morning. They hook up the camper and I leave before they pull out. I didn't want to watch the camper leave. When I return home later, the camper is gone; a chapter of my life closes. It's going on five years. I often think about those camping trips and all the fun we had with the camping families. Such wonderful memories and miracles were had by everyone.

Today I am on my way to town. I blow my horn and wave to a pickup truck pulling a camper. The feelings remain and I immediately want to call the camping families, pack and head out just one more time—even if it is by the seat of our pants.

Chapter Nineteen

Revelations by Ginger

I am packing for our beach trip today and it is very different. I'm packing the normal beach stuff like swimsuits, towels, sunscreen, umbrellas, but I'm not packing camping things. I'm packing the van and not the camper.

As we pull out of the driveway, I look back and the first wave of reality hits me. I miss the days of waking up at 3:00 a.m. to leave before it gets too hot to drive to St. Joe State Park and our three sleepy kids crammed in the tiny back seat. Camping with three kids with no air conditioning—not even a fan. What were we thinking? It was always the hottest week of the summer—or so it would seem. We fell in love with the beautiful isolated beach. We would return every year for the next thirty five years adding more camping families to our entourage.

Today, we travel the normal route in the van. Thirty five years ago we would leave at the same time and meet at the end of the road.

Later as the camping group grew in size we would meet in the K-Mart parking lot in Phenix City, Alabama. We arrive and line our campers up in the parking lot. Of course some of us would remember something we forgot or something we needed and we would run into K-Mart and shop. One of many stops we would make that day.

Today as we drive by K-Mart I look over and still see all those campers and the excitement of our group together. We sort of looked like a traveling circus family. Today we travel on freshly paved four lane roads and back then it was a narrow two-lane curvy, bumpy road with numerous bridges jolting the campers up and down. The kids thought it was a roller coaster ride.

There were few houses and certainly no stores between Phenix City and Eufaula, Alabama. We traveled together in case someone had problems, and believe me we always had problems. There were flat tires, radiators overheating, tires coming off the camper or bikes falling off the bike racks, you name it and we experienced it. We faced them together and always endured. We were a family and we still are a family. In fact we are known as "The Camping Families." When did all these stores and houses get built? There are Dollar

Generals in every little town now. I do not recognize some of the areas anymore.

As we approach Eufaula this morning, I see two eagles' nests with the mama eagles standing and watching over the babies in each nest. I am immediately reminded of how each of us must have looked as we stood on the beach watching over our babies. Funny how something so unrelated can trigger a memory from the past.

We pass the rest area where we always stopped on our way home for a bathroom break and also to hug and say our final goodbyes before we go in different directions home.

As we travel through the Historic District of Eufaula I still try to choose the southern antebellum mansion I want for my own. I can just see myself sitting on the beautiful front porch in a traditional long dress with three or four crinolines, a church fan in my hand, sipping my sweet iced tea and admiring the huge beautiful moss filled oak trees. Oh the many secrets and untold stories these houses and trees must shelter of yesteryear. On the other side of Eufaula (in later years) we always stopped at McDonald's for breakfast. My grandson, Ryan would not allow us to go by without stopping.

We travel on to Dothan and I see the big shiny steel pig that has become a landmark. It started out as a pig someone welded together out of bright shiny metal. Over the years they decided to paint it and make it the Crimson Tide mascot pig. I liked it better when it was just a regular pig. Of course, I am a Georgia Bulldog fan.

We pass the big flea market that on occasion we managed to talk the men into stopping so we could browse through the many aisles and tables of old rusty items we have plenty of but love to look through just in case we find that one must have treasure. I don't remember ever finding something but it was fun looking.

Just beyond the state line there is a house on the left that is so befitting of Florida. It has two huge beautiful oak trees with Spanish moss gently blowing in the wind. We knew we had arrived in Florida.

The next few miles are filled with acre after acre of farm land and churches on every corner. The small towns would have produce stands with locally grown tomatoes, watermelons and fresh boiled peanuts. Now most of the produce stands are gone and replaced with gas stations, hardware stories and Dollar Generals. Oh, how I miss the old days.

We make the turn toward Marianna and we know we're beginning the last leg of our trip. We pass the beautiful antebellum house with the huge curved front porch and I always said I wanted to stop and take a tour. It's a welcome center now and I haven't stopped but it's on my list of things to do.

We're approaching Wewahitchka where we always stopped to eat lunch. We would pull into the Church parking lot and make sandwiches. There were no fast food restaurants in this small town and this was our last stop before we got to Port St. Joe. From here there is nothing but long straight roads, farmland and trees. We would have to fight to stay awake.

Leaving Marianna, I start seeing the many—and I mean *many*—side roads that look familiar. This was the area that one of the campers would always experience some type of trouble or breakdown. We would pull down the side road and help the one in trouble. Sometimes it would only be a few minutes and other times we would pack the family in our trucks and return later for the camper or car. It became a ritual while the men worked on the problem the women would make snacks for the kids and sit on the shoulder of the road waiting.

As darkness falls, all of the families gather on the boardwalk to watch the sun go down over the water every night. We meet families that camp the same week we did every year. We would look for each a different sunset each night. It would signal the end of a glorious, fun-filled day. As we enter the city limits of Port St. Joe, I remember every Wednesday Nancy and I would come into town to wash clothes at the local laundromat. We would start the washing machines and then we would shop the five-and-dime-type stores down one side of the street; we turn around, go put the clothes in the dryers and finish shopping on the other side of the street. We were so excited when the state park put in a washer and dryer. I missed our shopping trip but the time we saved not having to drive into town was worth it. More time to spend on the beach.

When we saw the tall bridge over the waterway, we knew we were getting close to Port St. Joe. This is the place Mike, Dan and Richard decided they would go flounder gigging one night. I always wondered what prompted them to do that. Just three men having a fun filled experience, I assume.

We pass Wendy's where we would stop and eat lunch on our way home after we finally had enough money to enjoy such frivolities. When we turn on the road that leads toward the cape, I remember the old palm trees that grew right next to the road. I was right next to the road. I was always afraid we would hit one with the camper. Now they are gone too and the road has been resurfaced and improved.

We pass the area where we would park and walk out into the Gulf and snorkel for scallops. Originally we started our snorkeling adventures at the State park. I remember the first time I snorkeled. I was floating face down, just relaxing when I happened to float over a blow fish. It puffed up its ugly little body scaring me so bad I almost drowned in a foot of water. I almost remember finding my first scallop. It was sitting in the grass slightly open with his beautiful blue eyes looking at me, all of a sudden it spit and sputtered and I slung it half across the bay before I realized what I had done. It was gone. My first scallop was gone. What did I do?!

Later, we learned the scallops were more plentiful in the bay area near town and that is where we would drive and park on the roadside and walk a mile or two into the bay with nothing but kids and scallop nets. We were enthusiastic on the walk out but a few hours in the hot blazing sun with nothing to drink. We had nets full of heavy scallops and hungry tired kids. The walk back to the truck seems to take hours. After a few years we brought our jonboat and canoes—which made it easier.

Picking up the scallops is the fun part. We return to the park to eat a quick lunch and then take chairs and the scallop shells back to the marina to spend a few hours shucking scallops. The first time we tried opening the scallop's shells we didn't know how to do it. Thankfully someone saw our distress came over and showed us the proper way to use a scallop knife. Easy once you know how to do it.

Scalloping was just one of the many activities. The men love to fish in boats on the Gulf.

Today we reach our destination. We rent a house on the beach just a few miles from the State Park. The park is closed due to a powerful hurricane that hit the area earlier this year. The campground was an island for a while with the road completely washed away. We are told it will take years to rebuild.

After we settle in and unpack I go out and sit on the beach. I look down toward the old campground and my mind starts time traveling back to all the good times spent with such an amazing family of friends. We started out with our small children in tents. We upgraded to small campers, then larger campers to accommodate our children and grandchildren. Somewhere along the way the children grew up, got married and had children of their own, got campers of their own and started camping with us.

Generations of memories. Reminding me of a song, "And I think to myself, what a wonderful world." We may never "camp" together again, but we will have these memories that will remain with us forever. I am thankful for the times we shared then and for the new memories we continue to make.

Rebecca S. Carlisle

Acknowledgments

Sam Barham
Shea Carlisle
Lynda Petry

ABOUT THE AUTHOR

Rebecca S. Carlisle

Rebecca lives in Heard County, Georgia. She was an educator for forty-one years, serving as Principal of Ephesus Elementary before retiring. She is a Christian non-Fiction writer who has written six books since retiring. She has written articles for Lifetouch and Christian Focus Publishers.

Books

- Her First book, *52 Hats: A Memoir*, was about her Christian mother.
- Kidney Donation—*Sharing Lives: A Tale of Two Kidneys*
- *The Divine Touch: Thirteen Spectacular Accounts of Supernatural Healing*
- *The Legend of the Flying Machine*
- *A Legend in His Time: John W. Cox*
- *The Childersburg High School Football Coach Who Changed the World: John Cox*

Books available on Amazon.com

and Rebecca's website at:

rebeccacarlisle.com